The

Conversation

Piece

The
Conversation
Piece

*[Creative Questions
to Tickle the
Mind]*

**Paul Lowrie and
Bret Nicholaus**

Ballantine Books   New York

The second half of this book was originally published by
Questmarc Publishing in 1994.

http://www.randomhouse.com

Library of Congress Catalog Card Number: 96-96298

ISBN: 0-345-40711-3

Text design by Beth Tondreau Design

Manufactured in the United States of America

First Ballantine Books Edition: June 1996

12   13   14   15   16   17   18   19   20

Dedicated to the life and memory of

Al Nicholaus

We'll meet again

Acknowledgments

Christina Nicholaus
Randy Bray
Joseph Durepos, literary agent

Thanks to our Heavenly Father,
who provides joy in all of life's journeys

Introduction

The book you are holding, *The Conversation Piece*, has been designed with you, the reader, in mind. Every question has been thoughtfully created to stimulate the most exciting conversation possible. All you have to do is read a question aloud and watch the fun begin.

There is no order to the questions, so you may randomly select any question in the book at any time. Of course, you may follow the questions in numerical order if you wish.

Some of the questions that follow you may have thought about but never discussed. Others will be brand-new to you. However, unlike some other books, ours does not contain questions regarding serious personal beliefs and ethics that can lead to tension and discomfort within a group. *The Conversation Piece* is a real opportunity for you and others to answer thought-provoking questions while still having *fun*.

After a question has been read, we suggest that persons be given approximately 60 seconds to consider their answers. Some questions may require more time for reflection, some may require less.

Since many of the questions are hypothetical in nature, you may not know exactly what you would do if the stated situation were actually to occur. That's all right! Simply give the answer that you *believe* at that moment would be your course of action. (Your answer may change from day to day.) Feel free to reword the question if it's not clear to you at first.

Above all, have a good time! Answer the questions honestly, but creatively. *Elaborate on your answers whenever possible.* If you can cover 20 questions, great! If one question leads to a 30-minute conversation, that's great, too! Remember that this book was designed to make your conversations more creative, interesting, and exciting.

So what are you waiting for? Gather some people together and start asking questions!

The

Conversation

Piece

1

If you could fly in a hot-air balloon over any city in the world, what city would you choose?

2

Of all your favorite foods, which one would you find the most difficult to give up completely for the rest of your life?

3

You've been asked to design a zoological park for the future. How will you design this park to be radically different from the zoos of today? Be specific.

4

You've been given the chance to travel into the future to see how the world will change over the next 25 years. What change in particular are you most interested in?

5

While walking down a street in your neighborhood, you find a black briefcase clearly marked "Highly confidential information enclosed—do not open under any circumstances." What do you do?

6

More than likely, each of us has a favorite instrument, one whose sound we especially love. By the same token, we can probably name one instrument that we could easily do without. What instrument is *not* music to your ears?

7

Suppose you owned a large home in the country with a huge circular drive. If you could place any one thing in the center of that circle to greet your guests as they approached your home, what would it be?

8

What annually televised sporting event is an absolute must-see for you?

9

Suppose that each day you had to spend one hour in private meditation or contemplation and that by snapping your fingers, you could instantly transport yourself anywhere for the duration of this quiet time. Where would you choose to go?

10

How did they do that?! If you could learn the secret to any special effect or stunt from a popular movie, which one would you choose?

You're writing a mystery novel revolving around people who are disappearing one by one from a particular state in our country. The title, of course, is an important part of the success of the book. The catch: you must name the book after one of the 50 states (presumably, but not necessarily, the state from which the people are disappearing). Think marketing! Which state would you choose for the title of your book?

In your opinion, which animal is the most beautiful?

13

If you could be a part of any archeological dig, which one would it be?

14

If you were asked to make a "Top Ten" list of the people you regard as the all-time greatest Americans, whom would you rank first?

15

If you could have anything in the world
completely to yourself for one day—any
object or place—what would you choose?

16

If you were asked to design the ultimate
treehouse for the kids in your neighborhood,
what would you do to make the treehouse
stand out?

17

If you could have any building or institution
named after you, which one would you
choose?

18

Coffee and donuts, ham and cheese—a couple of classic combinations. What food and/or beverage combination is your personal favorite?

19

Okay, TV viewers: What's your all-time favorite commercial jingle?

20

If, through the use of a time machine, you could venture to any point in time in the future, how many years down the road would you want to travel?

21

You've been asked to conceive of a way to make the sport of baseball more interesting to watch. You can change the rules, the playing surface, the makeup of the teams, whatever you want, but you can only make *one* change. What will it be?

22

If you could add one month to the calendar year, inserting it between two existing months, where would you put your extra 30 days?

23

If you could somehow control the weather and add an additional season to the year, what would your new season be like?

24

Suppose for a moment that you are *truly* color-blind: all you can see is black and white. Then one day you wake up to find you can now see *one* color. Which color would you wish it to be?

25

If a movie producer decided to do a movie about your life, in which genre—e.g., romance, comedy, adventure—would people more than likely find it?

26

If you had to choose one icon to serve as the national symbol for the word *kindness*, what would it be?

27

If you could play a one-on-one game against any NBA player, against whom would you most want to "take it to the hoop"?

28

If you could listen to only one type of music for one full year, what type of music would you choose?

29

If you could have any book instantly memorized—cover to cover—which book would you choose?

30

You've just been given the chance to host your own late-night talk show. You need good ratings to stay on the air. What will you do to make your show unique?

31

Suppose you won $50,000—but had to give it all away. To which charity, cause, or institution would you donate it?

32

Through the use of a time machine, you are traveling back to the year 1850. You may take with you one, and only one, product or invention from the modern era. What would you take with you to impress and awe our forebears?

33

If you could be anywhere in the world for New Year's Eve 1999, where would you most want to be?

34

What is the greatest lesson in life you've ever learned?

35

If you had to describe your disposition in meteorological terms, what would a typical forecast be? (Example: Partly sunny with the chance of a sudden thunderstorm.)

36

For many people, bridges conjure up thoughts of romance, serenity, and beauty. In all your travels, what is the most memorable bridge you've ever crossed?

37

Besides something considered immoral or politically controversial, what is something that, if you did it, would shock the socks off the people who know you? (Example: If you hate sports, attending a football game.)

38

If you could design the ultimate firework to conclude your city's Fourth of July display, what kind of explosion would it make?

39

If you could acquire a characteristic of one particular animal, what would it be?

40

If you were backed by investors to create, introduce, and market a new sport throughout the world, what would it be?

41

You've been taken into a canyon. There you must shout out any one sentence you choose. Through the use of advanced technology, your shout and its echo will be bottled and sold throughout the country, to be heard every time someone opens one of the bottles. What words will you shout?

42

If you joined the circus, what act would you most want to perform?

43

On a tour of the Alaskan wilderness, what would you want to see more than anything else?

44

What is your favorite number—one through nine—and why?

45

If you had to move to a new part of the country, would you want to move north, south, east, or west of where you live now?

46

Suppose that you are in charge of coordinating a parade for your city or town. Who would you choose as the grand marshal?

47

Which famous person do you imitate or impersonate best?

48

If you could erect a lighthouse that would guide all human beings toward one particular virtue, which virtue would it be?

49

If you could buy any rare collection in the world, which would you choose?

50

If you lived on a farm, which chore above all others would you definitely prefer *not* to do?

51

What do you believe is the greatest unsolved mystery of all?

52

If you had to rearrange the letters of your first name to give yourself a new name, what would it be?

53

What one word or phrase do you wish people would say more often?

54

In your opinion, what is the most beautiful man-made object?

55

If you could hear a speech from the leading figure in any field, who would you choose to hear?

56

On a scale of one to ten, with one being totally dishonest and ten being honest to the penny, how truthful would you be if someone asked you how much money you make in a year?

57

What aspect of your daily routine do you look forward to the most?

58

What is the longest walk you've ever taken?

59

If a sculptor were making a statue of you, in what position would you like to be rendered?

60

Which unwieldy item would you most like to see made portable?

61

In your opinion, what is the funniest looking animal?

62

If you could wake up tomorrow morning fluent in any language, which language would you choose?

63

If you could walk into any painting and actually experience the moment it depicts, which painting would you choose?

64

If the door to your home could be made in any shape other than a rectangle, what shape would you want it to be?

65

When you were a child, what job did you most want to have when you grew up?

66

In your opinion, what is the best piece of music, pop or classical, ever written?

67

If you were writing and producing an action-adventure movie, where would you film it?

68

If you could design the pattern of the coat
of a new wild animal, what would it
look like?

69

If you were an entry in the dictionary,
under which word would people find you?

70

If you could change the custom of shaking
hands, what would you replace it with?

71

If you could add any new course to our nation's school curriculum, what would it be?

72

You are given a magic potion that allows you to be invisible for one hour and one hour only. What would you want to do during your hour of invisibility?

73

A major motion picture is being made about your life. What song or songs should be on the soundtrack?

74

If you could have one superpower, what would you want it to be?

75

If you could see the front page of a national newspaper dated January 1, 2100, what do you imagine the main headline might say?

76

What would the title of your autobiography be (not including your name)?

77

If you owned a clock shop, to what time would you set the hands on the clock faces? (Assume the clocks are not running and that they all must show the same time.)

78

Which daily activity do you perform with the greatest care?

79

What would your dream house look like? Be descriptive!

80

What do you think is the best conversation piece in your home?

81

Which of the seven dwarfs personifies you best—Dopey, Sneezy, Sleepy, Bashful, Grumpy, Happy, or Doc?

82

If you could stand at the pinnacle of any natural object or man-made structure, what would it be?

83

If something other than a cuckoo could pop out of a clock to announce the time, what would you want it to be?

84

If you were sent on assignment to rate the ten best small towns in America, what particular criterion would be most important to you?

85

If you had to choose one flower to wear daily in your hair or on your lapel, which flower would it be?

86

If you could travel back in time to meet anyone in your family's history, whom would you most want to meet?

87

If you could have a large stained-glass window in your home, what would you want it to depict?

88

Which particular historical document (or portion thereof) do you think every American should know by heart?

89

The good ol' general store. What particular candy would you insist on finding in a big jar at the counter?

90

Which of the three daily meals do you look forward to the most?

91

If you owned a pickup truck, what item would you regularly lug around in it?

92

If you had to describe your personality using a Native American name, what would it be?

93

The year is 2050; having a grass lawn is a thing of the past. What might have replaced the green stuff?

94

What is something you forgot once that you will *never* forget again?

95

You're working on a national advertising campaign to get people to eat more fish. What will your campaign slogan be?

96

If you could domesticate any wild animal, which animal would it be?

97

If you could create a new piece of furniture for your home, one that is not available in any store, what would it be?

98

If you were writing a new children's book, what might you choose for the setting and who might the main character be?

99

If you were to issue a new postage stamp, who or what would be on it?

100

If you could start another fad along the lines of the Pet Rock craze of the late 1970s, what inanimate object would you choose as the new "pet"?

101

What is the longest line you've ever stood in?

102

If you could bottle something in nature and sell it, what would you choose?

103

We're all familiar with frequent flyer programs. Suppose there was a similar program to reward you for something else you do frequently in your life. What would it be?

104

If you could take a train ride across any of the seven continents, which continent would you choose?

105

Sometimes whistles blow to warn us or get our attention. When would you most like to have a whistle blow to alert you?

106

A picture is worth a thousand words. What is one place you have seen that only a picture can adequately describe?

107

If you could add a new room to your house, what would it be?

108

Assume that cars don't exist—you must travel everywhere on your bicycle. What special feature would you want that bike to have?

109

If you had to come up with a practical alternative to business cards, what would it be?

110

If you could bring back any retired sports star, living or deceased, to play in one game, who would it be?

111

As unrealistic as it may seem, consider for a moment an alternative to war. What else might nations do to settle their differences?

112

If you could add anything at all to an elevator ride to make it more interesting, what would it be?

113

If you had to be trapped in a TV show for a month, which show would you choose? Consider the setting, the characters, the lifestyle, and so on.

114

You must develop a brand-new course to be taught in colleges. What will it be?

115

What is one item you own that you really should throw away . . . but probably never will?

116

If you could change or eliminate one wedding tradition, what would it be?

117

If you could eliminate one month on the calendar, going directly from the month preceding it to the month following it, which month would it be?

118

What special feature that doesn't yet exist would you like to see added to automobiles?

119

Which of the following places do you think would be the most fun to live in: a tree, a cave, or an underground burrow? Use your imagination.

120

If you had lived in the Old West, what do you think your occupation would have been?

121

If you could take a boat cruise on any river in the world, which river would you choose?

122

If you could change the traditional meal of Thanksgiving from turkey to another food, what would you choose?

123

You've probably heard the expression "They couldn't pay me enough to do that job." What job would that be for you?

124

If the temperature *had* to be the same on every day of the year, what would you want it to be?

125

If you could open your own retail store, what type of merchandise would you sell?

126

Suppose you were attending a costume party tonight. What or whom would you want to be?

127

If you could play any instrument at the professional level, what instrument would it be?

128

If you could avoid one household chore the rest of your life, what chore would it be?

129

If you had to describe your personality in terms of a farm animal, which animal would you choose?

130

If you could have your picture taken with any living person in the world today, with whom would you choose to be photographed?

131

If you had to choose your own epitaph of seven words or less (besides name and dates), what would it be?

132

If any *one* of the national holidays had to be celebrated twice a year, which one would you want it to be?

133

Suppose you were in charge of designing a building for a large U.S. city. What would you do to distinguish your building from the others?

134

If you could take any scent and bottle it as a perfume or cologne, what scent would you choose?

135

If you could have 50 pounds of anything other than money, what would you want?

136

If you could teach a dog any new trick, what would it be?

137

With so many new products on the market, it is becoming increasingly difficult to "keep up with the Joneses." What item do you lack that leads you to believe that you have fallen *behind* the Joneses?

138

If you opened a restaurant, what would be your house specialty?

139

If you won a contest in which your prize was to select any three guests for *The Tonight Show*, which three people would you choose?

140

If you were given 20 acres of land and the money to develop it however you chose, what would you do with it?

141

What is your favorite day of the year?

142

If you were on an African safari, what would you absolutely have to see for your trip to be complete?

143

If everyone were required to wear a hat at all times, what sort of hat would you wear?

144

If money were not a consideration, what do you believe would be the ideal number of children to have?

145

What do you think is the most soothing sound?

146

If you could catch the ball to make the last out in the seventh game of the World Series, how would you want to make that play?

147

If you could take any job for just one month, what job would you like to have? (Assume that you would have the knowledge to perform adequately.)

148

If you could be one inch tall for a day, what specific place would you most like to explore?

149

If your picture could be on the cover of any magazine in America, on what magazine would you want to be pictured and what great accomplishment would put you there?

150

What, for you, would have been the most discouraging aspect of living in the 1800s?

151

If you were asked to create the ultimate vacation destination, what would it be like and where would it be located?

152

What truly daring or courageous feat would you like to witness in person?

153

If you could create a new Hollywood monster, what would your monster look like and what would it do?

154

You've no doubt seen little children having fun at the playground. Assuming good health, what would *you* most enjoy doing at a playground?

155

Suppose you were asked to redesign the American flag. What changes would you make?

156

If you were a mail carrier, what kind of weather would bother you the most?

157

If you could move the celebration of Christmas from December 25 to a new date, what day would you choose?

158

What is your favorite saying, quote, or expression?

159

If you were completely blind but could somehow see for one hour each week, how would you spend that time?

160

If you won $2 million in tomorrow's lottery, what is the biggest effect it would have on your life? Be specific.

161

What is something you have not yet done that you believe you can accomplish during your lifetime?

162

If you could enter a race horse in the Kentucky Derby, what would you name your horse?

163

You are going to the beach for the day. Besides your swimsuit, you may take only *one* other item along with you. What would it be?

164

If you were an artist, what would be the theme of your drawings/paintings?

165

If you could own another home in addition to the one(s) you already have, where would you want it to be?

166

Suppose you could have the ability to compete in any Olympic event. In what event would you want to compete?

167

Almost everyone has something that he/she considers a sure thing. What is your "ace in the hole"?

168

I t is said that an apple a day keeps the doctor away. If you could select any food that, eaten every day, would keep the doctor away, what food would you choose?

169

W hat sound, other than ringing, would you like your telephone to make?

170

What would be the most enjoyable way for you to spend $25?

171

A visitor from abroad who has never been to the United States is coming to stay with you. What one place, attraction, or event would you be sure to take him or her to?

172

If it were commonplace for adults to play with children's toys, what toy would you most like to play with?

173

If you suddenly became a star and had to choose a stage name, what name would it be?

174

What task do you most often put off until tomorrow that you should do *today*?

175

If you could have been one of the early explorers of America, where would you have wanted to explore?

176

As the Christmas season approaches, what song is it that you just can't wait to hear?

177

What state in the Union would you be *least* interested in visiting?

178

What natural phenomenon or act of nature would you most like to see if you could witness it safely?

179

How would you redesign the dollar bill if you could?

180

If you could have "been there" to witness any specific moment in sports history, what moment would you choose?

181

What bit of knowledge/advice do you have that you wish you could pass on to everyone else?

182

What do you consider the ideal age to have a first child?

183

If sunset *had* to be at the same time every day of the year, what time would you want the sun to set?

184

What fear do you most want to be rid of forever?

185

Assume for a moment that your home is burning down. All the people and pets are safely outside and you have time to run back in to save *one* thing. What would you save?

186

If someone offered you a trip to any foreign country, where would you choose to visit?

187

Besides its intended purpose, what's the most creative way you can think of to use a paper clip?

188

If you could live anyone else's life for one month, *fully* experiencing their daily joys, sorrows, successes, and failures, whose life would you choose?

189

If you were given the money to build the world's greatest swimming pool, what would it be like?

190

If you and a partner had a free limousine at your disposal for one night, where would you most want to go?

191

If you could give any person a blue ribbon (other than a family member), to whom would you give it and why?

192

What event in American history that occurred during your lifetime do you most vividly remember?

193

If you were given 1,000 fresh roses, what would you do with them?

194

If you could take a "behind the scenes" look at anything, what would you most want to see?

195

What would be the ideal way for you to spend a hot Saturday afternoon in the middle of July?

196

If you could go back in time to witness any invention or discovery, what would you choose to see?

197

What's your favorite food to order when you eat at an upscale restaurant?

198

If you could channel your frustration whenever you became angry into any nondestructive activity, what would you choose to do?

199

Suppose you could eliminate television commercials but still had to fill the time slots. What would you choose to replace the commercials?

200

If you had a parrot and could teach it to say any word or short phrase, what would it be?

201

If *you* could set the hours of your 40-hour workweek, how would you distribute the time?

202

If you were an airline pilot and were told to choose any route that you would have to fly for your entire career, what two cities would your flight connect?

203

If you could see to it that one magazine was on every coffee table in America, what magazine would you choose?

204

If you could be any age again for one week, what age would you be?

205

Which of the four seasons do you most anticipate?

206

If you were to write a book, what would you choose as the topic?

207

If you could go back in time to safely witness any battle in world history, which battle would you choose to see?

208

Everyone at work has been asked to place an ornament on the company Christmas tree that best represents him/herself. What would *your* ornament look like?

209

What is one event in the future whose outcome you would like to know *now*?

210

If you could have two front-row tickets to see any singer or musical group, whose concert would you attend?

211

If you were asked to create the ultimate dessert, what would it be?

212

If you could proclaim a new national holiday, what would it be and how would we celebrate it?

213

What is something that you enjoy that is a chore for most other people?

214

You must choose a movie to show at a party attended by many adults from different backgrounds and lifestyles. What movie would you choose to show?

215

What world record would you most want to establish?

216

If you could invite anyone in the world to your house for dinner, whom would you invite and what would you serve them?

217

You must bury a time capsule to be opened 200 years from now. What three items would you put in the capsule to give people an idea of life in the 1990s?

218

What particular sound annoys you the most?

219

What animal would you most like to house in your backyard, if you could?

220

You can design any new ride or attraction for Walt Disney World. What will it be?

221

What is an item that you own that has a minimal monetary value but has such sentimental value that you would not sell it for $5,000?

222

On a scale of one to ten (with one being very uneasy and ten being very comfortable), how comfortable would you feel delivering a 15-minute speech to an audience of 200 people?

223

If you could be the spokesperson for any product on the market, what product would you choose to represent?

224

What is the most exciting event you've ever witnessed?

225

If you had to substitute-teach for two months, which grade (kindergarten through twelfth) would you choose to teach?

226

If you had one hour each day to relax *completely*, what would you want to do for that hour?

227

What object, place, or attraction would you classify as the greatest "wonder of the world"?

228

If it were socially acceptable for you to dress for work any way you liked, what would be your typical outfit?

229

If you owned a yacht, what would you name it?

230

If you could be remembered for any act of bravery, what would it be?

231

If you could be any inanimate object for a day, what would you be?

232

If you could be "home for the holidays" with family and friends anywhere in the world, where would you want to be?

233

Which month of the year do you *least* anticipate?

234

What "moment of glory" have you watched another person celebrate that you too would love to experience?

235

What do you consider the ideal household income for a family of four?

236

At what local, regional, or national event would hearing "The Star-Spangled Banner" be most meaningful for you?

237

If drinking fountains could dispense another liquid, what would you want it to be?

238

What is the most interesting course you have ever taken in school?

239

If you could appear as a guest star on any television show, which show would you choose?

240

If you had only enough time each day to read *one* section of the newspaper, which section would you choose to read?

241

If you could go back in time and somehow avert any tragedy in American history, what incident would you choose to prevent?

242

If you were chosen to be a participant in the Rose Bowl Parade simply because of who you are, in what type of vehicle would you most like to ride?

243

If you had $15 to spend at the ballpark, how would you spend it? (Assume you would not have to pay for your ticket or parking.)

244

If you were a migrating bird, where would you fly for the winter?

245

Everyone hears discussions that they consider boring. What topic can put *you* to sleep more quickly than any other?

246

What item that you don't currently possess would you most like to have in your home?

247

If you could have a memento of any famous person, what would you want it to be?

248

Besides the usual horse and dog races, what type of animal race do you think would be interesting to watch? (Assume the animals would be treated well.)

249

Which food would you rank first on you list of *least* favorite foods?

250

The U.S. government has asked you to pick another animal in addition to the eagle to depict America. What animal would you choose?

251

If you could have a window view from your office in a 100-story building, what floor would you want to be on?

252

If you were completely deaf but were somehow able to hear for one hour each week, what would you want to hear for that hour?

253

If Christmas were tomorrow, what gift would you want most?

254

On a scale of one to ten (with one being very comfortable and ten being very uneasy), how uneasy would you feel sitting between two strangers on an airplane?

255

If you *had* to change your first name, what would you choose as your new name?

256

If you had to wear a button with a maximum of five words on it describing your outlook on life, what would your button say?

257

In a spelling bee, what word would you hope you would *not* have to spell?

258

What specific aspect of being a child do you miss the most?

259

What is the most beautiful drive you've ever taken? Be as descriptive as possible.

260

Of all the movie *characters* you've seen, which one do you believe is most like you?

261

What, for you, would have been the most exciting aspect of living in the preceding century? Be specific.

262

What do you believe the fine should be for running a red light? Assume the light has been red for several seconds.

263

What outdoor scent do you enjoy more than any other?

264

For a literally sensational experience, you have been offered the chance to jump off a diving board into a pool filled with *anything* of your choice. Into what substance would you want to jump?

265

Suppose your dream NBA Championship or Super Bowl could be realized. What two teams would be playing each other and which team would you root for?

266

If you were given an unlimited amount of money and the necessary technology to invent anything you desired, what would you invent?

267

What specific subject do you feel you know better than any other subject?

268

You are walking alone at night on a suburban street when a man wearing a black mask confronts you and demands your money. It does not appear that he is carrying a weapon, but you do not know for certain. How do you respond?

269

If you could create and market a toothpaste in any flavor besides mint, what new flavor would you choose?

270

Suppose you could be on vacation with pay for the entire summer. Also assume that someone offered to pay for any summer adventure you could imagine. Where would you choose to go and what would you do?

271

If you were given a $50 gift certificate to spend in any store, where would you choose to redeem it?

272

What thought or sentiment would you like to put in one million fortune cookies?

273

What is one of the simple pleasures of life you truly enjoy?

274

If you could invent a pair of glasses that would allow you to see abstract things (e.g., the motives behind someone's actions), what would you want to see?

275

As a form of punishment, children are sometimes deprived temporarily of something they cherish. If you were going to be punished in this way as an adult, what item would you least want to lose? (Assume the deprivation would last one month.)

276

What is something that most people consider a modern-day convenience that you consider a pain in the neck?

277

If you could break or smash any object against a brick wall whenever you needed to release frustration, what object would you choose?

278

If you were invited to a dinner party, what hors d'oeuvre would you most want to find on the table?

279

If you had a great voice and were given a contract to record an album, what style of music would you sing?

280

Suppose you lived in a house surrounded by acres of trees. What particular type of tree would you want flourishing on your land?

281

You've seen signs that say No Smoking, No Pets, No Trespassing, etc. If you could put an original "No _____ " sign on your front door, what would it say?

282

If you could have a scale model of anything you wanted, what would it be?

283

If you could speak for one minute by phone to anyone living in the world, who would it be?

284

If you could go to a land of make-believe for one day, what would you most want to experience?

285

If you could own a sweatshirt that advertised any place in the world, what would it promote?

286

Most people have a story or experience that they love to share with other people. Here's your chance. What's *your* story?

287

If you could be one of America's "most wanted," but wanted because of some *skill* you have, what great skill would you want to possess?

288

How much money would a person have to pay you to spend one night alone in an old mansion that is supposedly haunted?

289

If you could find out only *one* fact about every person you met, what fact would you want to know?

290

If neither time nor money were an issue, what do you think would be the most enjoyable way to travel from New York to California?

291

If you could have the *original* of anything, what would you want it to be?

292

If you could carve your name in stone anywhere in America, where would you do it?

293

If you had a personal maid or butler who would perform only *one* task a day for you, what job would you choose to have her/him do?

294

If you were given $2,000 to put toward anything of your choice, how would you spend the money?

295

If you could go back in time and live through any five-year period in history, what period would you choose?

296

When you consider nature and/or creation, what do you stand most in awe of?

297

In what field of endeavor would you most want to take a two-hour crash course?

What would an island paradise be like for you? Describe it in detail.

If you *really* wanted to upset your dentist, what would you eat immediately before having your teeth cleaned?

300

If, like a product, your behavior came with a guarantee, what could you *honestly* guarantee about yourself?

301

If you were told that you could watch only *one* television show a week for one year, what show would you choose to watch?

302

Which sport would you most like to play professionally?

303

If you could create a memorial to yourself in a city park, what would it be?

304

If you were a member of a national public relations staff, what spectacular event would you like to stage in celebration of the Fourth of July?

305

If you could go back in time and relive any moment in your life exactly as it originally happened, what event would you choose to experience again?

306

You have two choices:

1. You may live in a region where the day and nighttime temperature is always between 80 and 90 degrees Fahrenheit, or . . .

2. You may live in a region where the day and nighttime temperature is always between 40 and 50 degrees Fahrenheit.

Which would you choose?

307

If you could write a sequel to any movie, what movie would it be?

308

If you had to have the same topping on your vanilla ice cream for the rest of your life, what topping would you choose?

309

By how many hours would you lengthen the 24-hour day to allow yourself enough time to do everything you need to do?

310

If you were asked to create the ultimate candy bar, what would it be like?

311

You are offered an envelope that you know contains $50. You are then told that you may either keep it or exchange it for another envelope that *may* contain $500 or *may* be empty. Do you keep the first envelope or do you take your chances with the second?

312

If you could wake up every morning and look out your bedroom window at the perfect view, what would that view be?

313

If you were offered a 60-second spot during prime-time television to say or promote anything you wanted, how would you use this time?

314

Assume that you are stranded for one month on an uninhabited tropical island that *does* have shelter and plenty of food and water. What one item would you want with you on the island?

315

What national attraction or tourist site should every American see at least once?

316

If you could go back in time and ask any famous person in history one question, whom would you question and what would you ask? (Assume you would be given an honest answer.)

317

If you could experience something considered very dangerous with your safety guaranteed, what would you want to experience?

318

Almost everyone can recall a missed photo opportunity because he/she did not have a camera. What moment above all others do you wish you could have caught on film?

319

On a scale of one to ten (with one being very relaxing and ten being very stressful), how stressful is your job?

320

If you could add any question to this book, what would it be?

About the Authors

Paul Lowrie and **Bret Nicholaus** are
1991 graduates of Bethel College, St. Paul,
Minnesota. They hold their degrees in
marketing and public relations/advertising,
respectively. Both authors firmly believe that
creative questioning is the key to truly
learning about ourselves and others.